The Lord's Prayer

A Pattern for Powerful Prayers

*An In-Depth Look into the Outline of Prayer
as Taught by Jesus to His Disciples and How We Can Break
It Down into Targeted Points of Prayer in Our
Daily Time of Communion with the Father*

DENNIS E. BOS

ISBN 979-8-88616-889-1 (paperback)
ISBN 979-8-88616-890-7 (digital)

Christian Faith Publishing
832 Park Avenue
Meadville, PA 16335
www.christianfaithpublishing.com

Scripture quotations are taken from the following sources as noted in the text:
1. Amplified Bible Classic (AMPC). Copyright 1954, 1958, 1962, 1964, 1965, 1987 by the Lockman Foundation. Used by permission (www.lockman.org)
2. New King James Version (NKJV). Copyright 1982 by Thomas Nelson Inc. Used by permission. All rights reserved
3. King James Version (KJV) (public domain)

Words and definitions from the original Greek are sourced from Strong's and Thayer's using the Blue Letter Bible app via https://www.blueletterbible.org/:
1. *Strong's Exhaustive Concordance* (public domain)
2. *Thayer's Greek Lexicon* (public domain)

Printed in the United States of America

CONTENTS

PREFACE

For many, that which has been traditionally known as the Lord's Prayer has become a ritual, rote prayer of convenience and repetition in religious practice.

Over the years I have heard many different teachings on prayer, and there are many great books and resources available to give guidance and insight into prayer, in its different aspects and types. There are books on devotional prayer, intercessory prayer, petitioning and spiritual warfare, and prayer for healing and prayer of faith.

However, recently my pastor, Pastor Blaine Herron, at Emmanuel Foursquare Church in Salina, Kansas, was teaching on the four living creatures of Revelation. In one message, entitled "The Lion: Prayer and Warfare," he referenced characteristics of prayer and warfare in the Lord's Prayer. For the next couple of days after his message, I spent time reflecting upon the things he shared and letting the Holy Spirit lead and guide me into deeper revelation and understanding of the Lord's Prayer, building upon my own study in prayer, dating back over the past forty years. So over a period of a few hours, it was as if I received a divine upload of the outline for what would become this book.

In Luke 11:1 (NKJV) we see Jesus, as was His custom, going apart from the crowds to spend time in prayer or communion with the Father. And *one of His disciples said to Him, Lord teach us to pray, as John also taught his disciples.*

We must understand these disciples were raised in the Jewish customs of worship and prayer in the synagogues under the priests, the scribes, and the Pharisees and Sadducees. They were not accustomed to prayer on the level of intimacy as they observed in Jesus's life. God was not viewed or spoken of or spoken to on a level of familial or intimate terms, as they saw in Jesus's life. Jesus was bringing new revelation and teaching that must have seemed strange in comparison to what was taught and observed in the temple or synagogue worship where much ritual was present. God was seen as unapproachable except through the sacrifices and offerings and the annual atonement for their sins with the blood of bulls and goats, which was taken by the high priest, once a year, into the holy of holies before the ark of the covenant to the mercy seat to cover over their sins for a year.

But now, Jesus was teaching and modeling and demonstrating to the people an entirely new concept, that of God as a Father, whom they could approach on a personal level in intimate communion and fellowship to make their petitions known to Him as their Father.

I have heard it taught that this prayer is not for believers of the new covenant but was a prayer for the disciples still living under the old covenant. But as we saw earlier, Jesus had come to reveal God as our heavenly Father and bring a new revelation of our relationship to God, as a Father-and-son relationship, which is actually looking forward to the new covenant in which we are no longer servants of God but sons and daughters born anew into the family of God. 1 John 3:1 (NKJV) says, *Behold what manner of love the Father has bestowed on us, that we should be called the children of God.*

So then, this pattern or outline that Jesus taught to the disciples is very much for new covenant believers as sons and daughters of the heavenly Father.

Now, let us begin our study of this prayer commonly referred to as the Lord's Prayer.

CHAPTER 1

Paternity

Let's begin by looking at the background leading up to Jesus's teaching His disciples this pattern or outline of prayer in Matthew 6. Just prior to this, Jesus had been teaching what is referred to as the "Sermon on the Mount" in chapters 5, 6, and 7 of Matthew.

In chapter 6 Jesus was contrasting giving and prayer as it should be to that which was practiced by the religious leaders whom Jesus called "hypocrites," who were full of pride and religious works but whose hearts were far from God.

So, in Matthew 6:5–13 (NKJV), Jesus said

> *And when you pray, you shall not be like the hypocrites. For they love to pray standing in the synagogues and on the corners of the streets, that they may be seen by men. Assuredly, I say to you, they have their reward.*
>
> *But you, when you pray, go into your room, and when you have shut the door, pray to your Father Who is in the secret place; and your Father Who sees in secret will reward you openly.*
>
> *And when you pray, do not use vain repetitions as the heathen do. For they think that they will be heard for their many words.*

> *Therefore do not be like them. For your Father knows the things you have need of before you ask Him.*
>
> In this manner, therefore, pray: Our Father in heaven, Hollowed be Your name.
>
> *Your kingdom come. Your will be done on earth as it is in heaven.*
>
> *Give us this day our daily bread.*
>
> *And forgive us our debts, as we forgive our debtors.*
>
> *And do not lead us into temptation, but deliver us from the evil one. For Yours is the kingdom and the power and the glory forever. Amen.* (emphasis mine)

So now let's begin to break this down and look at it more closely. Matthew 6:9 (NKJV) says: *Our Father in heaven.* The first thing we see here then is the concept of *paternity.* God is not just some distant, uninterested, unapproachable Creator Who is disengaged from us. We don't take away from Him as being a holy God and Creator and Sovereign, the King and Lord of all things, but we understand here a new revelation and concept of God as our loving, personal heavenly Father. Jesus referred to this leading up to the model or pattern of prayer He would reveal to the disciples. In verse 6 He said, *But you, when you pray, go into your room, and when you have shut the door, pray to your Father Who is in the secret place; and your Father Who sees in secret will reward you openly.*

First is the idea of this new relationship to come through Jesus in the new covenant: the idea of God as our Father and us as His dear and beloved children. Note Jesus said we are to go into our room or inner chamber and shut the door. This is a picture of privacy and intimacy, as a child with their father. This is private, family business and interaction or communion taking place. This is not a conversation for public display and show.

It reminds me of my own daughter, who at the time of this writing is twelve years old, who at the end of the day, at bedtime, often in the quiet and peace before sleep, wants to talk and tell me about her day. Sometimes she asks questions about God and Jesus and the Bible or about things she has encountered in school that she thinks are contrary to biblical teachings. It is not a public conversation, and often things she wants to share or ask of me are things she doesn't want anyone else to know, sometimes not even other members of the family. These are things she just wants to tell me or ask my advice or thoughts or opinion on but doesn't want me to ever tell anyone else. It is a personal and intimate relationship between a child and a parent that God, as our Father, wants us to share with Him.

In Psalm 91:1–2 (AMPC), it says

> *He who dwells in the secret place of the Most High shall remain stable and fixed under the shadow of the Almighty [Whose power no foe can withstand (or resist)].*
> *I will say of the Lord, He is my Refuge and my Fortress, my God; on Him I lean and rely, and in Him I [confidently] trust! [And I shall not be afraid!]*

This is that place of safety and refuge we have as children of God. In the beginning, in the garden of Eden, Adam had perfect communion with the Father. It was a closeness that was lost in the fall of man when Adam sinned, which Jesus came to restore and reveal to us.

Second, note Jesus said: *when you pray*. The word in the original Greek for pray is *proseuchomai*. It is a compound of the words

- *Pros*: Meaning "toward, forward, or a position and state of looking toward a thing." You could say this is face-to-face.
- *Euchomai*: Meaning "to pray, to speak."

So we see then this is an intimate conversation or prayer looking toward God as our Father. Or you could say it is a face-to-face encounter or conversation with the One with Whom you are in an intimate relationship.

Third, Jesus said in verse 8: *for your Father knows the things you have need of before you ask Him.* Note the word *ask* in this verse. It is another Greek word for prayer or petition, which is another type or dimension of prayer within that time of intimate communion with the Father.

Here, the word for "ask" is *aiteo*, which means "to ask, beg, crave, desire, or require" and is normally from the position of an inferior making petition of one in a superior position and carries with it the idea of placing a demand or requiring a thing based upon that intimate relationship as a right.

Next, note Jesus said here: *the Father knows what we have need of before we ask.* This shows us the heart of the Father. He has already thought of and provided for all things we could ever have need of before we even ask or even know we have the need. In Genesis 1, in the creation story, we see that the Father anticipated everything mankind would ever have need of, even in a fallen condition, before He created man. So He first created and provided all things in abundance that mankind would ever have need of for all human history.

Before God created Adam (man) in Genesis 1:26, God had placed everything in creation that man could or would ever have need of.

Then, in verses 28–29 (AMPC), it says

> *And God blessed them and said to them, be fruitful, multiply, and fill the earth, and subdue it [using all its vast resources in the service of God and man]; and have dominion over the fish of the sea, the birds of the air, and over every living creature that moves upon the earth.*
>
> *And God said, see, I have given you every plant yielding seed that is on the face of all the land and every tree with seed in its fruit; you shall have them for food.*

God didn't create man first and then when Adam was hungry say, "Oh, here let Me create something for food for you." No, just like we as parents provide for our children, God as our Creator and Father anticipated and provided all things all mankind, throughout all history, would ever need.

In Matthew 7:7–11 (NKJV), it says

> *Ask, and it will be given to you; seek, and you will find; knock, and it will be opened to you.*
>
> *For everyone who asks receives, and he who seeks finds, and to him who knocks it will be opened.*
>
> *Or what man is there among you who, if his son asks for bread, will give him a stone?*
>
> *Or if he asks for a fish, will he give him a serpent?*
>
> *If you then, being evil, know how to give good gifts to your children, how much more will your Father who is in heaven give good things to those who ask Him!*

Looking back to Matthew 6:8–9, Jesus said then, since our Father knows before we ask what we have need of, *implying He has already made provision for all we have need of,* therefore, because He has already provided all things, *ask*! Like a child who asks for whatever they desire of their parents, we are to ask or pray, in that place of intimate, face-to-face communion with the Father, for all that we have need of, with the awareness of God as our heavenly Father, who loves us and cares for us and has already provided all things we could ever need or desire.

He is our Father. We are not born of corruptible seed but incorruptible seed, by the Word of God, and we have a *paternal* Father Who loves us and delights to provide everything we have need of and all our hearts' desire when we delight in Him.

CHAPTER 2

Position

In chapter 1 we saw the paternal relationship of God to us as His children when we come to Him through Jesus Christ our Lord and Savior. We saw He is more than just Creator and God; He is a Father to us.

Looking further then in this verse, we see it says: *Who is in heaven.* This speaks of *position*!

In Ephesians 1:17–2:7 (AMPC), it reads

> *[For I always pray to] the God of our Lord Jesus Christ, the Father of glory, that He may grant you a spirit of wisdom and revelation [of insight into mysteries and secrets] in the [deep and intimate] knowledge of Him,*
>
> *By having the eyes of your heart flooded with light, so that you can know and understand the hope to which He has called you, and how rich is His glorious inheritance in the saints (His set-apart ones),*
>
> *And [so that you can know and understand] what is the immeasurable and unlimited and surpassing greatness of His power in and for us who believe, as demonstrated in the working of His mighty strength,*

Which He exerted in Christ when He raised Him from the dead and seated Him at His [own] right hand in the heavenly [places],

Far above all rule and authority and power and dominion and every name that is named [above every title that can be conferred], not only in this age and in this world, but also in the age and the world which are to come.

And He has put all things under His feet and has appointed Him the universal and supreme Head of the church [a headship exercised throughout the church], [Ps. 8:6]

Which is His body, the fullness of Him Who fills all in all [for in that body lives the full measure of Him Who makes everything complete, and Who fills everything everywhere].

And you [He made alive], when you were dead (slain) by [your] trespasses and sins

In which at one time you walked [habitually]. You were following the course and fashion of this world [were under the sway of the tendency of this present age], following the prince of the power of the air. [You were obedient to and under the control of the [demon] spirit that still constantly works in the sons of disobedience [the careless, the rebellious, and the unbelieving, who go against the purposes of God].

Among these we as well as you once lived and conducted ourselves in the passions of our flesh [our behavior governed by our corrupt and sensual nature], obeying the impulses of the flesh and the thoughts of the mind [our cravings dictated by our senses and our dark imaginings]. We were then by nature children of [God's] wrath and heirs of [His] indignation, like the rest of mankind.

But God—so rich is He in His mercy! Because of and in order to satisfy the great and wonderful and intense love with which He loved us,

Even when we were dead (slain) by [our own] shortcomings and trespasses, He made us alive together in fellowship and in union with Christ; [He gave us the very life of Christ Himself, the same new life with which He quickened Him, for] it is by grace (His favor and mercy which you did not deserve) that you are saved (delivered from judgement and made partakers of Christ's salvation).

And He raised us up together with Him and made us sit down together [giving us joint seating with Him] in the heavenly sphere [by virtue of our being] in Christ Jesus (the Messiah, the Anointed One).

He did this that He might clearly demonstrate through the ages to come the immeasurable (limitless, surpassing) riches of His free grace (His unmerited favor) in [His] kindness and goodness of heart toward us in Christ Jesus. (Emphasis mine)

Notice in chapter 1, verse 17, that Paul, writing by inspiration of the Holy Spirit, said: *the God of our Lord Jesus Christ, the Father of glory, that He may grant you a spirit of wisdom and revelation [of insight into mysteries and secrets] in the [deep and intimate] knowledge of Him.* So again we see that intimacy of relationship with the Father.

Then he spoke of Jesus being raised from the dead and being seated at the Father's own right hand in heavenly places. This *position* in the heavenly, spiritual realm is

Far above all rule and authority and power and dominion and every name that is named [above every title that can be conferred], not only in this age and in the world, but also in the age and the world which are to come. And the Father has put all things

> *under Jesus's feet and appointed Him the universal*
> *and supreme Head of the church, which is His body.*

Then in chapter 2, verse 6, he said: *And He raised us up together with Him and made us sit down together [giving us joint seating with Him] in the heavenly sphere [by virtue of our being in Christ Jesus.*

2 Corinthians 5:17 (AMPC) says, *Therefore if any person is [ingrafted] in Christ (the Messiah) he is a new creation (a new creature altogether); the old [previous moral and spiritual condition] has passed away. Behold the fresh and new has come.*

Again, in 1 John 3:1 (AMPC), he said, *See what [an incredible] quality of love the Father has given (shown, bestowed on) us, that we should [be permitted to] be named and called and counted the children of God!*

Just as Jesus arose victorious and has been exalted and raised and is seated at the right hand of the Father, so we, too, in Christ, have our *position* in the heavenlies, seated at the right hand of the Father. We have been placed in a *position* of dominion above principalities, powers, the rulers of darkness of this world, and spiritual wickedness in high places in this age and world and in the age and world to come.

As Jesus is, so are we in this world, as we are told in 1 John 4:17. And again, in 1 John 4:4, it says we are more than conquerors and overcomers in Christ because *greater is He that is in us than he that is in the world.*

1 John 5:4 (AMPC) says, *For whatever is born of God is victorious over the world; and this is the victory that conquers the world, even our faith.*

In Hebrews 10:19–23 we see we have freedom and confidence to enter the Holy of Holies into that secret chamber or place of intimate fellowship by the power and virtue of the blood of Jesus. It is by this fresh, new, and living way, which the Father initiated for us to enter through the veil that is through His flesh. Therefore, by our relationship (*paternity*) and *position* in Christ, we can draw near and come boldly, having our hearts sprinkled and purified from a guilty conscience. It says in Romans 8:1–2 (NKJV)

> *There is therefore now no condemnation to those who are in Christ Jesus, who do not walk according to the flesh, but according to the Spirit.*
> *For the law of the Spirit of life in Christ Jesus has made me free from the law of sin and death.*

So just as our Father is seated upon His heavenly throne, in and through Christ Jesus, *positionally*, we are seated with Him and have dominion restored, through Christ Jesus, just as Adam had in the beginning.

CHAPTER 3

Praise

So we've discovered paternity and *position* within the Lord's Prayer, so let us now move into the element of *praise*.

Let's continue in Matthew 6:9 (AMPC): *Hallowed [kept holy] be Your name.*

This speaks to us of our attitude of *praise* and worship, our reverence and awe of God in His holiness.

In Psalm 100:4 (NKJV), it says: *Enter into His gates with thanksgiving, And into His courts with praise. Be thankful to Him, and bless His name.*

Isaiah 6:1–4 (NKJV) says

> *In the year that King Uzziah died, I saw the Lord sitting on a throne, high and lifted up, and the train of His robe filled the temple. Above it stood seraphim; each one had six wings: with two he covered his face, with two he covered his feet, and with two he flew. And one cried to another and said: "Holy, holy, holy is the Lord of hosts; The whole earth is full of His glory!" And the posts of the door were shaken by the voice of him who cried out, and the house was filled with smoke.* (emphasis mine)

Revelation 4:1–11 (AMPC) says

> *After this I looked, and behold, a door standing open in heaven! And the first voice which I had heard addressing me like [the calling of] a war trumpet said, Come up here, and I will show you what must take place in the future.*
>
> *At once I came under the [Holy] Spirit's power, and behold, a throne stood in heaven, with One seated on the throne! [Ezek. 1:26]*
>
> *And He Who sat there appeared like [the crystalline brightness of] jasper and [the fiery] sardius, and encircling the throne there was a halo that looked like [a rainbow of] emerald. [Ezek. 1:28]*
>
> *Twenty-four other thrones surrounded the throne, and seated on these thrones were twenty-four elders (the members of the heavenly Sanhedrin), arrayed in white clothing, with crowns of gold upon their heads.*
>
> *Out from the throne came flashes of lightning and rumblings and peals of thunder, and in front of the throne seven blazing torches burned, which are the seven Spirits of God [the sevenfold Holy Spirit];*
>
> *And in front of the throne there was also what looked like a transparent glassy sea, as if of crystal. And around the throne, in the center at each side of the throne, were four living creatures (beings) who were full of eyes in front and behind [with intelligence as to what is before and at the rear of them]. [Ezek. 1:5, 18]*
>
> *The first living creature (being) was like a lion, the second living creature like an ox, the third living creature had the face of a man, and the fourth living creature [was] like a flying eagle. [Ezek. 1:10]*
>
> *And the four living creatures, individually having six wings, were full of eyes all over and*

within [underneath their wings]; and day and night they never stop saying, Holy, holy, holy is the Lord God Almighty (Omnipotent), *Who was and Who is and Who is to come. [Isa. 6:1–3]*

And whenever the living creatures offer glory and honor and thanksgiving to Him Who sits on the throne, Who lives forever and ever (through the eternities of the eternities), [Ps. 47:8]

The twenty-four elders (the members of the heavenly Sanhedrin) fall prostrate before Him Who is sitting on the throne, and they worship Him Who lives forever and ever; and they throw down their crowns before the throne, crying out,

Worthy are You, our Lord and God, to receive the glory and the honor and dominion, for You cre-ated all things; by Your will they were [brought into being] and were created. [Ps. 19:1]

In these passages of scripture, we get just a small glimpse of our Father's holiness and majesty that produces awe and wonder and worship to all who encounter His presence.

Psalm 99:3 (NKJV) says, *Let them praise Your great and awesome name—He is holy.*

Psalm 99:5 (NKJV) says, *Exalt the Lord our God, And worship at His footstool—He is holy.*

Proverbs 9:10 (AMPC) says, *The reverent and worshipful fear of the Lord is the beginning (the chief and choice part) of Wisdom, and the knowledge of the Holy One is insight and understanding.*

1 Samuel 2:2 (AMPC) says, *There is none holy like the Lord, there is none besides You; there is no Rock like our God.*

Psalm 103:1 (NKJV) says, *Bless the Lord, O my soul; And all that is within me, bless His holy name!*

There is much more we can see in Scripture concerning God's holiness and our coming to Him with *praise* and thanksgiving, so take time to search out what His Word has to reveal to us. Look into and study the "seven redemptive" names of our Father and Yeshuwah our Lord. He is worthy of all our *praise,* and we should call to remembrance Who He is and all He has done in our times of prayer and communion with Him—for He is holy, righteous, and altogether lovely and worthy of *praise.*

CHAPTER 4

Prophesy

As we continue on in Matthew 6:10 (AMPC), it says, *Your kingdom come, Your will be done on earth as it is in heaven.*

Here we come into agreement with our Father's plans, purposes, and pursuits for our lives; our families; our cities, states, and nations; and the world. It is here we *prophesy* and declare what God has already decreed in heaven, even before the foundations of the earth.

Isaiah 55:8–11 (AMPC) says

> *For My thoughts are not your thoughts, neither are your ways My ways, says the Lord.*
>
> *For as the heavens are higher than the earth, so are My ways higher than your ways and My thoughts than your thoughts.*
>
> *For as the rain and snow come down from the heavens, and return not there again, but water the earth and make it bring forth and sprout, that it may give seed to the sower and bread to the eater, [2 Cor. 9:10]*
>
> *So shall My word be that goes forth out of My mouth: it shall not return to Me void [without producing any effect, useless], but it shall accomplish that which I please and purpose, and it shall prosper in the thing for which I sent it.*

Now let's look at 1 Corinthians 2:10–16 (AMPC):

Yet to us God has unveiled and revealed them by and through His Spirit, for the [Holy] Spirit searches diligently, exploring and examining everything, even sounding the profound and bottomless things of God [the divine counsels and things hidden and beyond man's scrutiny].

For what person perceives (knows and understands) what passes through a man's thoughts except the man's own spirit within him? Just so no one discerns (comes to know and comprehend) the thoughts of God except the Spirit of God.

Now we have not received the spirit [that belongs to] the world, but the [Holy] Spirit Who is from God, [given to us] that we might realize and comprehend and appreciate the gifts [of divine favor and blessing so freely and lavishly] bestowed on us by God.

And we are setting these truths forth in words not taught by human wisdom but taught by the [Holy] Spirit, combining and interpreting spiritual truths with spiritual language [to those who possess the Holy Spirit].

But the natural, nonspiritual man does not accept or welcome or admit into his heart the gifts and teachings and revelations of the Spirit of God, for they are folly (meaningless nonsense) to him; and he is incapable of knowing them [of progressively recognizing, understanding, and becoming better acquainted with them] because they are spiritually discerned and estimated and appreciated.

But the spiritual man tries all things [he examines, investigates, inquires into, questions, and discerns all things], yet is himself to be put on trial and judged by no one [he can read the meaning of everything, but no one can properly discern or appraise or get an insight into him].

For who has known or understood the mind (the counsels and purposes) of the Lord so as to guide and instruct Him and give Him knowledge? But we have the mind of Christ (the Messiah) and do hold the thoughts (feelings and purposes) of His heart *[Isa. 40:13].* (Emphasis mine)

Notice here in verse 16 it says that we have the mind of Christ and we do hold the thoughts (feelings and purposes) of His heart. Back in Isaiah it said our thoughts are not His thoughts and our ways are not His ways, yet in the new birth, 2 Corinthians 5:17–18 tells us that for any person who is in Christ and is a new creation and whose old spiritual condition is passed away, all things have become new. And that "all things," that is, that new spiritual condition or man, is from God, who through Jesus Christ received us into favor and brought us into harmony with Himself. This is so that now we hold His thoughts and purposes in our new man, that is, in our heart or innermost being. That old heart of stone that was dead in trespasses and sin is passed away, and we have been given a new heart of flesh.

In Galatians 2:20 (NKJV), the apostle Paul said: *I have been crucified with Christ; it is no longer I who live, but Christ lives in me; and the life which I now live in the flesh I live by faith in the Son of God, who loved me and gave Himself for me.*

1 Corinthians 6:19 (NKJV) says, *Or do you not know that your body is the temple of the Holy Spirit who is in you, whom you have from God, and you are not your own?*

So now, the Holy Spirit dwells in us. We have the spirit of Christ, and in that new spirit in us, we have the mind of Christ. We hold the thoughts and intents and purposes of the Father within our spirit, but we must renew our natural minds with God's Word. We tap into that spiritual flow from our innermost being as we seek His face, praying in the spirit.

Jude 1:20 (NKJV) says, *But you, beloved, building yourselves up on your most holy faith,)praying in the Holy Spirit.*

In 1 Corinthians 14:2 (AMPC) we see, *For one who speaks in an [unknown] tongue speaks not to men but to God, for no one understands or catches his meaning, because in the [Holy] Spirit he utters secret truths and hidden things [not obvious to the understanding].*

In verse 4a he said, *He who speaks in a [strange] tongue edifies and improves himself.*

Then in verses 13–15 he said

> *Therefore, the person who speaks in an [unknown] tongue should pray [for the power] to interpret and explain what he says.*
>
> *For if I pray in an [unknown] tongue, my spirit [by the Holy Spirit within me] prays, but my mind is unproductive [it bears no fruit and helps nobody].*
>
> *Then what am I to do? I will pray with my spirit [by the Holy Spirit that is within me], but I will also pray [intelligently] with my mind and understanding; I will sing with my spirit [by the Holy Spirit that is within me], but I will sing [intelligently] with my mind and understanding also.*

In conjunction with these verses, we see in Romans 8:26–28 (AMPC) it says

> *So too the [Holy] Spirit comes to our aid and bears us up in our weakness; for we do not know what prayer to offer nor how to offer it worthily as we ought, but the Spirit Himself goes to meet our supplication and pleads in our behalf with unspeakable yearnings and groanings too deep for utterance.*
>
> *And He Who searches the hearts of men knows what is in the mind of the [Holy] Spirit [what His intent is], because the Spirit intercedes and pleads [before God] in behalf of the saints according to and in harmony with God's will. [Ps. 139:1, 2]*

> *We are assured and know that [God being a partner in their labor] all things work together and are [fitting into a plan] for good to and for those who love God and are called according to [His] design and purpose.*

So from these passages, we see all the treasures of divine wisdom. His thoughts and purposes are stored up in us when we were born anew into His family, and the spirit of Christ and the mind of Christ dwell in us. But our natural minds have not undergone complete redemption and transformation and renewal, so we must be *constantly renewed in the spirit of your mind* (Eph. 4:23). Romans 12:2b (AMPC) says: *but transformed (changed) by the [entire] renewal of your mind [by its new ideals and its new attitude], so that you may prove [for yourselves] what is the good and acceptable and perfect will of God.*

In Jude and Corinthians, we saw we were to "build ourselves up" praying in the Holy Spirit. And when we pray "in the spirit," we edify ourselves. This is a picture, spiritually, of building up our spirit in our most holy faith. But even more, it speaks to repairing or replenishing that which is broken or missing in our whole being—spirit, soul, and body. In our fallen condition, our natural mind (soul) and our spirit were severed from the spirit and the mind or thoughts of our Father. But in the new birth, our spirit is reborn, quickened, and made alive by the Holy Spirit. And as we pray in the spirit, expecting Him to speak to and through us, He will take the things concerning Jesus and reveal them to us. He, the spirit of truth, will lead and guide us into all the truth. Then we can pray not only with the spirit, as the Apostle Paul said, but with the understanding as the Holy Spirit gives us a fresh revelation and insight into the circumstance about which we pray, so that we might speak God's Rhema Word into that situation.

Then, as God declared and decreed in heaven and spoke His Word into the earth and into our lives by His Word and His Holy Spirit, we can then take His Word and declare it in the earth, in our lives, in our circumstances, and over our bodies, our families, and our finances. And His Word will accomplish that for which He sent it. And it shall not return unto Him void, empty, or without producing any effect, for His Word is alive and quick and powerful and sharper than any two-edged sword and contains within itself the power to bring it to pass. (See Hebrews 4:12 [AMPC or NKJV].)

So we declare or *prophesy* His kingdom will be established in the earth and His thoughts, purposes, plans, and pursuits brought about in our lives as He has decreed in heaven from before the foundations of the earth.

CHAPTER 5

Provision

Let's continue on in Matthew 6:11 (NKJV): *Give us this day our daily bread.*

In Matthew 6:25–34 (KJV), Jesus spoke to the disciples about all the things that the world worries about and stresses over and contrasted that with the birds of the air and the lilies of the fields and how the Father feeds and takes care of them and that we are more valuable than they and will He not, much more, take care of His children. Then in verse 31 (KJV) He said, *Therefore take no thought, saying, What shall we eat? Or, What shall we drink? Or, Wherewithal shall we be clothed?* Note: He said *take no thought, saying…* Don't take ownership of thoughts that exalt themselves against the knowledge of God and His Word. We'll look at this more in chapter 7.

We already have seen that the Father has made provision of all things we would ever have need of. So then the obvious question might be "Why do we need to ask?"

Remember, in the garden of Eden, Adam had everything richly, lavishly, and abundantly supplied and there was no lack of anything he could ever have need of and no toil required of him to partake of it. But then when Adam sinned and partook of the one thing that God had reserved for Himself (the tithe unto God), his connection and communion with God was severed. This one tree in the midst of the garden was Adam's tithe of all that God had provided, and by reaching forth and taking of it, it was not only an act of disobedience—it was an act of robbing God of the tithe. (See Malachi 3:8–11.)

Now Adam had a new connection to *Satanas,* the accuser of the brethren, who now became Adam's new lord and master. Now, Adam had given his legal dominion and authority over God's creation, which God had entrusted to him, to Satan. And now God's provision was no longer freely available but was under new management. That new management, the devil, is a thief and liar and has come to steal, to kill, and to destroy.

So now, as long as mankind's term of dominion and management over God's creation is in effect, God must have the agreement of a man in the earth to intervene in the affairs of mankind.

Some might say, "But God is Sovereign and can do whatever pleases Him." But God is just and true and cannot lie. Therefore, God cannot and will not violate His Word or covenant.

Psalm 89:34 (NKJV) says, *My covenant I will not break, Nor alter the word that has gone out of My lips.*

Matthew 24:35, Mark 13:31, and Luke 21:33 all say: *Heaven and earth will pass away, but My words will by no means pass away.*

Numbers 23:19 (NKJV) says: *God is not a man, that He should lie, Nor a son of man, that He should repent. Has He said, and will He not do? Or has He spoken, and will He not make it good?*

Psalm 138:2 (NKJV, emphasis mine) says: *I will worship toward Your holy temple, And praise Your name For Your lovingkindness and Your truth;* For You have magnified Your word above all Your name.

But thanks be to our heavenly Father. He sent His Son, Jesus the Anointed One, to redeem us back to the Father. He has translated us out from the dominion and control of the kingdom of darkness and into the kingdom of light and life in Christ Jesus, our Lord.

1 John 3:8 (NKJV) says: *He who sins is of the devil, for the devil has sinned from the beginning. For this purpose the Son of God was manifested,* that He might destroy the works of the devil.

Thank God Jesus came to destroy, to annihilate, and to bring to nothing and put out of business the works of the devil, that is, the deceiver. The devil's power and authority over our lives has been rendered null and void in Christ Jesus.

Colossians 2:15 (NKJV) says: *Having disarmed principalities and powers, He made a public spectacle of them, triumphing over them in it.*

Colossians 2:14–15 (AMPC) says

> *Having cancelled and blotted out and wiped away the handwriting of the note (bond) with its legal decrees and demands which was in force and stood against us (hostile to us). This [note with its regulations, decrees, and demands] He set aside and cleared completely out of our way by nailing it to [His] cross.*

[God] disarmed the principalities and powers that were ranged against us and made a bold display and public example of them, in triumphing over them in Him and in it [the cross].

Colossians 1:19–20 (NKJV) says

> *For it pleased the Father that in Him all the fullness should dwell, and by Him to reconcile all things to Himself, by Him, whether things on earth or things in heaven, having made peace through the blood of His cross.*

Matthew 28:18–20 (NKJV) says

> *And Jesus came and spoke to them, saying, "All authority has been given to Me in heaven and on earth.*
>
> *Go therefore and make disciples of all the nations, baptizing them in the name of the Father and of the Son and of the Holy Spirit, teaching them to observe all things that I have commanded you; and lo, I am with you always, even to the end of the age." Amen.*

So now, Jesus told us, since the Father knows all that we have need of, even before we ask, and since He already made *provision* for all things lavishly and in abundance, as His children, redeemed from the curse, we can *ask* or declare His *provision* to be released into our lives and know without any reservation that it is His will to richly supply all our need and, yes, even our wants and desires as we delight in Him. (See Psalm 34:9–10 and Psalm 37:4.)

Now, our daily bread doesn't just include our food and the other necessities of life, such as transportation, housing, clothing, etc. It is much more than that!

2 Peter 1:2–3 (KJV) says

> *Grace and peace be multiplied unto you through the knowledge of God, and of Jesus our Lord, according as his divine power hath* given unto us all things that pertain unto life and godliness, *through the knowledge of him that hath called us to glory and virtue.* (Emphasis mine)

3 John 1:2 (AMPC) says: *Beloved, I pray that you may prosper in every way and [that your body] may keep well, even as [I know] your soul keeps well and prospers.*

He said here *that you may prosper in all things and be in health, just as your soul prospers"* (NKJV).

Let's look over in Matthew 15:22–28 (NKJV) at the story of the Canaanite woman who came to Jesus:

> *And behold, a woman of Canaan came from that region and cried out to Him, saying, "Have mercy on me, O Lord, Son of David! My daughter is severely demon-possessed."*
>
> *But He answered her not a word. And His disciples came and urged Him, saying, "Send her away, for she cries out after us."*
>
> *But He answered and said, "I was not sent except to the lost sheep of the house of Israel."*

> *Then she came and worshiped Him, saying,*
> *"Lord, help me!"*
>
> *But He answered and said, "It is not good to*
> *take the children's bread and throw it to the little*
> *dogs."*
>
> *And she said, "Yes, Lord, yet even the little dogs*
> *eat the crumbs which fall from their masters' table."*
>
> *Then Jesus answered and said to her, "O*
> *woman, great is your faith! Let it be to you as you*
> *desire." And her daughter was healed from that very*
> *hour.*

Notice Jesus said to the Canaanite woman that being healed or receiving healing and release from demonic oppression is the children's bread. I believe that should settle the question as to whether or not it is God's will to heal you. But we are told in Scripture that everything should be established in the mouth of two or three witnesses. So let us look at two other passages of scripture to settle if it is God's will that we be healed.

Matthew 8:2–3 (NKJV) says

> *And behold, a leper came and worshiped Him,*
> *saying, "Lord, if You are willing, You can make me*
> *clean."*
>
> *Then Jesus put out His hand and touched him,*
> *saying, "I am willing; be cleansed." Immediately his*
> *leprosy was cleansed.*

The leper said to Jesus, "Lord, if You're willing"—or "if You will." And Jesus not only reached out and touched him. He emphatically stated, "I will"! Remember Jesus said that He only did and said what He heard the Father say and saw the Father do and that in fact it was not Jesus doing the work, the miracles, and the healing but it was the Father in Him Who did the works.

Now let's look at Acts 10:38 (NKJV), which says: *how God anointed Jesus of Nazareth with the Holy Spirit and with power, who went about doing good and healing all who were oppressed by the devil, for God was with Him.*

It was God, the Father, who anointed Jesus with the Holy Spirit and with healing virtue or power to heal and to set free *all* who were being oppressed by the devil.

God is not schizophrenic!

He is not double-minded and divided in His opinions. His kingdom is not divided against itself. He is not putting sickness and disease on you to teach you some spiritual lesson or to somehow "give God glory" through your suffering.

No!

Jesus bore all our suffering—our diseases, pains, and sorrows—upon His own body on the cross that we might have life and that life more abundantly!

But you must tap into all God's *provision* for your life—spirit, soul, and body. When you pray, expect and declare that divine health and healing, as a child of God, are part of your "daily bread" and God wants to richly supply all your need.

CHAPTER 6

Pardon

Now we come to Matthew 6:12 (NKJV), which says: *And forgive us our debts, As we forgive our debtors.*

First, let's settle that this is not about our salvation here in this outline of prayer for the believer. This is a prayer pattern or outline for those who are already in the family of God, those who are the "children of God." If you have gotten this far and are not certain if you have ever been born anew into God's family as a son or daughter, then take a moment to do so right now.

Romans 10:8–13 (NKJV) says

> *But what does it say? "The word is near you, in your mouth and in your heart" (that is, the word of faith which we preach):*
>
> *that if you confess with your mouth the Lord Jesus and believe in your heart that God has raised Him from the dead, you will be saved.*
>
> *For with the heart one believes unto righteousness, and with the mouth confession is made unto salvation.*
>
> *For the Scripture says, "Whoever believes on Him will not be put to shame."*

> *For there is no distinction between Jew and Greek, for the same Lord over all is rich to all who call upon Him.*
>
> *For whoever calls on the name of the Lord shall be saved.*

If you have never done this, pray this prayer right where you are, believing and trusting in God by faith. And He will hear and answer your prayer. He will give you a new heart (spirit), and the spirit of Christ will dwell in you whereby you can cry out, "Abba, Father":

"God, I come to You humbly confessing that I am a sinner but believing that You sent Jesus to be the sacrifice for me and bear my sin upon the cross. I believe He suffered and died, for my sin, but that You raised Him up from the dead. I confess now, with my mouth, that Jesus is my Lord and Savior. Now I proclaim You, God, as my Father. And I confirm my salvation, for You said if I believe in my heart that You raised Jesus from the dead and confess with my mouth that He is Lord, I would be saved. So right now, Father, I thank You. I am a new creation in Christ Jesus, and I ask You to baptize me and fill me with Your Holy Spirit and give me power to be Your witness and to speak with new tongues. In Jesus's name I pray, amen."

Now, let's take a look at this verse here concerning forgiveness of sins and trespasses.

In 1 John 1:8–9 (NKJV) we read

> *If we say that we have no sin, we deceive ourselves, and the truth is not in us.*
>
> *If we confess our sins, He is faithful and just to forgive us our sins and to cleanse us from all unrighteousness.*

During our daily lives, we still are dealing with the old nature of the flesh and the influence of the world in our unrenewed minds. This is why it is important daily to spend time in reading and studying God's Word coupled with prayer to be constantly renewing our minds. But we all stumble and fall; we all sin from time to time. But as we grow and mature in grace and in His Word, that should be an occurrence that happens less and less frequently. But when we do miss it, when we do say or do or dwell on a line of thought that is wrong, we should not run from God but immediately run to Him as our loving heavenly Father because He has already dealt with the "sin" problem.

He is not keeping an account of handwriting against us but was personally present in Christ reconciling us back to Himself. Our relationship is not severed when we miss it. Just like a child or even a puppy, who has done something wrong, who is ashamed and hangs their head and doesn't want to look their parent or master in the eye, our own hearts condemn us and interrupt our fellowship with the Father. But Romans 8:1 (NKJV) tells us: *There is therefore now no condemnation to those who are in Christ Jesus, who do not walk according to the flesh, but according to the Spirit.*

Christ Jesus does not condemn us but restores us, and the Father is quick to forgive and cleanse us (our conscience) of all unrighteousness. It is the enemy, that old serpent and snake, the devil, who is a deceiver and the accuser who condemns us. But we *overcome him by the blood of the Lamb and the Word of our testimony.* (See Revelation 12:10–11.)

Now let's look at the latter part of verse 12, which says: *as we forgive those who trespass against us* or *our debtor.*

Look with me now at Matthew 16:19 (NKJV, emphasis mine): *And I will give you the keys of the kingdom of heaven, and* whatever you bind on earth will be bound in heaven, and whatever you loose on earth will be loosed in heaven.

Let's also look at a parallel passage over in Matthew 18:15–22 (NKJV):

> *Moreover if your brother sins against you, go and tell him his fault between you and him alone. If he hears you, you have gained your brother.*
>
> *But if he will not hear, take with you one or two more, that "by the mouth of two or three witnesses every word may be established."*

> *And if he refuses to hear them, tell it to the church. But if he refuses even to hear the church, let him be to you like a heathen and a tax collector.*
>
> Assuredly, I say to you, whatever you bind on earth will be bound in heaven, and whatever you loose on earth will be loosed in heaven.
>
> *Again I say to you that if two of you agree on earth concerning anything that they ask, it will be done for them by My Father in heaven.*
>
> *For where two or three are gathered together in My name, I am there in the midst of them.*
>
> *Then Peter came to Him and said, "Lord, how often shall my brother sin against me, and I forgive him? Up to seven times?"*
>
> *Jesus said to him, "I do not say to you, up to seven times, but up to seventy times seven."*
> (Emphasis mine)

So notice the common phrase in these two passages of scripture: *whatever you bind on earth will be bound in heaven, and whatever you loose on earth will be loosed in heaven.*

Before we study out this phrase, let's look at the word translated as "keys" leading up to Jesus's statement above. Jesus said, *I will give you the keys of the kingdom of heaven.* Here we see the word *keys* in the Greek is the word *kleis* (Strong's G2807). The Thayer's Greek Lexicon definition reads: "a key." Since the keeper of the keys has the power to open and to shut, the word *kleis* is figuratively used in the New Testament to denote power and authority, of various kinds— also, referring to "the power of David [who is a type of Messiah, the second David], i.e., of receiving into Messiah's kingdom and of excluding from it."

So we see here this is granting of a power and authority to open or shut, to permit or to disallow something. So let's look closer now at the words translated here from the Greek text: *to bind* and *to loose.*

"To bind" is from the Greek word *deo* (Strong's G1210) and is a primary verb: "to bind [in various applications, literally or figuratively]: -bind, be in bonds, knit, tie, wind." This word can be used either in a negative sense, as to bind up in chains, to forbid or prohibit. Or it can be used in a positive sense as in to "knit together," to bind together as in a covenant agreement, to repair a breech. However, historically, this word, *deo*, is always seen as being in the positive sense when used in context opposite of a negative as we see in both these passages of scripture where it is opposite the word translated "to loose."

"To loose" is from the Greek word *lyo* (Strong's G3089) pronounced [luo] or [loo-o], meaning "to 'loosen' [literally or figuratively]: -break(up), destroy, dissolve, (un)loose, melt, put off"—also, to overthrow, do away with, or put out of business as seen in 1 John 3:8: *for this purpose was the Son of God manifest, to destroy the works of the devil.*

So here in Matthew 16 we see Jesus grant "the keys of the kingdom" that is the authority and power "to bind," that is, knit together those whose fabric of life has been torn apart from God through sin and restore them or reconcile them to God by virtue of the gospel message through the gospel of Christ and the preaching of the death, burial, and resurrection of Jesus. 2 Corinthians 5:18–20 (paraphrased) says we have been given *the ministry of reconciliation,* that is, that God was in Christ reconciling the world to Himself and has *committed to us the word of reconciliation. Now then we are ambassadors for Christ, as though God were pleading through us: we implore you on Christ's behalf, be reconciled to God.*

We also have the power "to loose" or dissolve or disallow. Here we can use that power or authority to loose demonic powers from their assignments over our lives and affairs. We have authority to forbid and disallow their activity in our bodies, our lives, our family, and our home. We also can dissolve fellowship with disobedient believers who will not submit to the authority of the Word and repent of an offense. Remember, in Matthew 18:15–22, the context was a brother who had wronged you. We are instructed to go to them and show them their fault, in love. And if after all the attempts to reconcile them, they refuse to listen, even to the church leadership, then we are to sever fellowship with them. Jesus said, *For truly I tell you, whatever you bind on earth shall be bound in heaven and whatever you loose* [dissolve or disallow] *shall be loosed in heaven.*

He then went on to say in verse 19 (AMPC): *Again I tell you, if two of you on earth agree [harmonize together, make a symphony together] about anything.* What two was He talking about? The two who had ought between them. If your brother listens and you are reconciled, your fellowship is restored, and not only have you knit the fabric of that fellowship between you back together but you have knit the fabric of his fellowship in the body of Christ back together and restored him; and whatever you ask in symphony or harmony together will be granted by the Father, and that brother's fellowship is restored in the kingdom.

In James 5:19–20 He said

> *Brethren, if any of you do err from the truth, and one convert him; let him know, that he which converteth the sinner from the error of his way shall save a soul from death, and shall hide a multitude of sins.*

There are further examples of this in scripture, such as when the apostle Paul stated that he had turned a fellow believer "over to Satan for the destruction of the flesh" that in the end his soul might be preserved and saved.

When I come to this portion of the outline in prayer, I always give thanks to God that His Holy Spirit has shed abroad in my heart the love of God that I may be merciful and quick to forgive others, just as God in Christ has forgiven me. There are many other references throughout the epistles that command us to be kind, forgiving and loving toward one another, longsuffering, and patient and forbearing with one another's faults and weaknesses.

CHAPTER 7

Protection (Warfare)

Matthew 6:13 (NKJV) says: *And do not lead us into temptation, But deliver us from the evil one.*

James 1:12–15 (AMPC) says

> *Blessed (happy, to be envied) is the man who is patient under trial and stands up under temptation, for when he has stood the test and been approved, he will receive [the victor's] crown of life which God has promised to those who love Him.*
>
> *Let no one say when he is tempted, I am tempted from God; for God is incapable of being tempted by [what is] evil and He Himself tempts no one.*
>
> *But every person is tempted when he is drawn away, enticed and baited by his own evil desire (lust, passions).*
>
> *Then the evil desire, when it has conceived, gives birth to sin, and sin, when it is fully matured, brings forth death.*

1 Corinthians 10:13 (AMPC) says

> *For no temptation (no trial regarded as enticing to sin), [no matter how it comes or where it*

leads] has overtaken you and laid hold on you that is not common to man [that is, no temptation or trial has come to you that is beyond human resistance and that is not adjusted and adapted and belonging to human experience, and such as man can bear]. But God is faithful [to His Word and to His compassionate nature], and He [can be trusted] not to let you be tempted and tried and assayed beyond your ability and strength of resistance and power to endure, but with the temptation He will [always] also provide the way out (the means of escape to a landing place), that you may be capable and strong and powerful to bear up under it patiently.

So as you pray, thank God that He does not tempt you with evil nor is He tempted with evil, but with every temptation, He is faithful and has made a way of escape in the temptation. He has given us weapons of spiritual warfare that are not carnal but mighty through His spirit to overcome in every temptation.

2 Corinthians 10:3–6 (AMPC) says

For though we walk (live) in the flesh, we are not carrying on our warfare according to the flesh and using mere human weapons.

For the weapons of our warfare are not physical [weapons of flesh and blood], but they are mighty before God for the overthrow and destruction of strongholds,

[Inasmuch as we] refute arguments and theories and reasonings and every proud and lofty thing that sets itself up against the [true] knowledge of God; and we lead every thought and purpose away captive into the obedience of Christ (the Messiah, the Anointed One),

Being in readiness to punish every [insubordinate for his] disobedience, when your own submis-

sion and obedience [as a church] are fully secured and complete.

2 Corinthians 10:4–5 (KJV) says it this way:

> *(For the weapons of our warfare are not carnal, but mighty through God to the pulling down of strong holds;)*
> *casting down imaginations, and every high thing that exalteth itself against the knowledge of God, and <u>bringing into captivity every thought</u> to the obedience of Christ.*

So, in the KJV it says, *casting down imaginations*. Or I like to say it like this: "vain imaginations and worthless or empty fantasies." In the AMPC it says, *[Inasmuch as we] refute arguments and theories and reasonings and every proud and lofty thing that sets itself up against the [true] knowledge of God and we lead every thought and purpose away captive into the obedience of Christ.*

In Ephesians 6:10–18 (KJV) we read

> *Finally, my brethren, be **strong** in the Lord, and in the power of his might.*
> *Put on the whole armour of God, that ye may be able to stand against the wiles of the devil.*
> *For we wrestle not against flesh and blood, but against principalities, against powers, against the rulers of the darkness of this world, against spiritual wickedness in high places.*
> *Wherefore take unto you the whole armour of God, that ye may be able to withstand in the evil day, and having done all, to stand.*
> *Stand therefore, having your loins girt about with truth, and having on the breastplate of righteousness;*

*and your feet shod with the preparation of the
gospel of peace;*

*above all, taking the shield of faith, wherewith
ye shall be able to quench all the fiery darts of the
wicked.*

*And take the helmet of salvation, and the
sword of the Spirit, which is the word of God:*

*praying always with all prayer and supplica-
tion in the Spirit, and watching thereunto with all
perseverance and supplication for all saints.*

We see in verse 10 we are to be *strong in the Lord and in the
power of His might.* In Luke 24:49b (KJV, emphasis mine) He said:
but tarry ye in the city of Jerusalem, until ye be endued *with power from
on high.* We see here it says they were to wait to be "endued" with
power, and this is the same word in the Greek as in Ephesians 6:10:
"to be strong" in the Lord. It means to be clothed upon, like a man-
tle. It is an enduement of power and ability to do what one could not
normally do. Jesus said in John 14 that what He said, He did not say
on His own authority or His own accord, but "the Father Who lives
continually in Me does the works." So it is with us, that enduement
from on high that empowers us, the anointing within and upon that
strengthens us in every temptation and battle. Ephesians goes on to
say we are to put on God's whole armor that we may be able to stand
up against the "wiles of the devil." In 2 Corinthians 2:11 (NKJV) it
says, *lest Satan should take advantage of us; for we are not ignorant of
his devises.* Satan is the accuser and is cunning and uses deceit and lies
to deceive us.

Here the word *devises* is the Greek word *noema* but comes from
the root word *noeo*, which means to "exercise the mind." *Noema* is
a perception, purpose, devise, or thought. So putting this together,
we see Satan tries to trick us with perceptions and thoughts, reasonings, and imaginations to exercise our mind against the true
knowledge of God. Looking back in Ephesians 6:11, it said we are
to be armed with the whole armor of God that we may be able "to
stand against the wiles of the devil." The word *wiles* here is from the

Greek word *methodeia* (Strong's G3180) and is a compound word from *meta* (Strong's G3326), a preposition meaning "with" as used here, and *hodeuo* (Strong's G3593), meaning "to travel," and comes from the root word *hodos* (Strong's G3598), meaning "a road; by implication, a progress; figuratively, a mode or means: of travel." So taken together it is seen as a method of operation, a well-worn path, an avenue always traveled or an MO. When put together with 2 Corinthians 2:11, we see Satan has one road or avenue of attack, one method whereby he lies in wait to deceive—and that is with the exercising of the mind with anxieties, worries, vain imaginations or fantasies, or tormenting thoughts that burn into your mind with the express purpose to deceive. We further see this born out in his title here as "the devil," which is from the compound word in the Greek *Diabolos*, which comes from the root word *Diaballo*, which is also a compound word from *dia* (Strong's G1203), a preposition denoting "the channel of an act; through" (or you could say it is a way through something or to pierce or penetrate something), and *ballo* (Strong's G906), meaning "to throw (more of less violently or intensely)." So *Diabolos* means to throw something violently or intensely like a javelin with the express purpose or intention to pierce or penetrate to deceive.

This is the picture of the enemy bombarding your mind with flaming missiles or fiery darts of tormenting thoughts that inflame and burn in your mind with the purpose to penetrate and pierce through in order to deceive. Therefore, take up God's whole armor that you may successfully stand in the face of the attacks of the enemy.

Looking back at Matthew 6:31a (KJV), we saw Jesus said, *take no thought, saying.* Often we have thoughts that we assume are just from our own minds, but in reality we have no original thoughts in and of ourselves. We may be presented with thoughts from God, by His Holy Spirit. Or thoughts may come to us from the "world, the flesh, and the devil." And these thoughts generally fall under the categories of the "lust of the flesh," "lust of the eyes," or "pride of life." The Amplified Classic Bible says it like this: *For all that is in the world—the lust of the flesh [craving for sensual gratification] and the lust of the eyes [greedy longings of the mind] and the pride of life [assur-*

ance in one's own resources or in the stability of earthly things]—these do not come from the Father but are from the world [itself].

So, now that we know there are thoughts that are constantly being presented to our minds by outside sources, we must always be on guard as we see in 2 Corinthians 10 and Ephesians 6 and lift the shield of faith, taking on the whole armor of God and being endued with the power of His might, and take a stand firm against the constant "mind games" and bombardment of thoughts that "exalt themselves against the knowledge of God" and not take ownership of those thoughts by "saying" them but rather "cast down those thoughts and imaginations and reasonings and bring them into captivity to the obedience of Christ." And be assured the enemy is ever ready to use our words against us. When we take those thoughts that "exalt themselves against the knowledge of God," we then give Satan place and authority to "steal, kill, and destroy" in our lives. On the other hand, when we cast down those thoughts and take God's Word and declare it over the temptation, trial, or testing, we give God's Word place to work in our lives to deliver us and cause us to triumph over every temptation, test, and trial.

Unfortunately, many believers and entire denominations within the church have laid aside much of God's armor. Yes, they have the "helmet of salvation," and many still have their "feet shod with the preparation of the gospel of peace, but the belt of truth is loose and frayed and not securely fastened so their "breastplate of righteousness" has fallen by the wayside. Without their "belt of truth" securely fastened, they have not accepted all the truth of God's Word of power and provision for their spiritual walk and warfare. And sadly, their shield of faith has not been kept well-oiled through the oil of anointing of the Holy Spirit and saturated with the water of the Word to extinguish the flaming, fiery darts of the enemy. They have never taken up the sword of the spirit, which is the "Rhema" Word of God—that fresh inspired, quickened Word of God that the spirit wields. They are walking around in their daily walk with their helmet and shoes on, while the rest of their spiritual armor is cast aside and they are otherwise spiritually naked before the enemy and exposed to his attacks.

Here in Ephesians, it says we can successfully stand; the word here means to place oneself in a position to stand firm, immovable.

In this passage in verses 11 and 12, every time we see the word *against*, it is not from the Greek word meaning "anti." But rather it is the word *pros* (Strong's G4314) from the root word *pro* (Strong's G4253), meaning a primary preposition—fore, that is, in front of. Or Thayer's Greek Lexicon says, "before (the face of) one. So pros is a strengthened form of the preposition of direction, forward or toward, denoting direction toward a thing. Or we could say then we are to take a position to stand firm in the face of the enemy's attacks. We are in a close-combat encounter, face-to-face with principalities, powers, the rulers of darkness of this world (system), and spiritual wickedness in high places, in a life-or-death struggle against the devil's strategies and deceits. But verse 13 (AMPC) says: *Therefore put on God's complete armor, that you may be able to resist and stand your ground on the evil day [of danger], and, having done all [the crisis demands], to stand [firmly in your place].*

This tells us here that with God's "complete armor" we are able to "resist and stand." This means to oppose, to press against and push away something with all effort. It goes on to say, "having done all [the crisis demands] to stand [firmly in your place]." We are to bring to a conclusion and stand in a place of victory holding our ground with firm, sure-footed stability.

James 4:7 (NKJV) says: *Therefore submit to God. Resist the devil and he will flee from you.*

1 Peter 5:8–9 (KJV) says

> *Be sober, be vigilant; because your adversary the devil, as a roaring lion, walketh about, seeking whom he may devour:*
> *whom resist stedfast in the faith, knowing that the same afflictions are accomplished in your brethren that are in the world.*

Verse 6 says: *Humble yourselves therefore under the mighty hand of God, that he may exalt you in due time.*

So we humble ourselves before God, taking unto us God's complete armor. We actively *resist* the devil's attacks, his fiery darts, by lifting the shield of faith. Faith comes by hearing and hearing by the Word of God (Romans 10:17). We take up the sword of the spirit, which is the Word (Rhema) of God, that Word which the Holy Spirit quickens unto us in that place of resistance in prayer that we might disable the enemy's onslaught and bring every contrary thought and circumstance into the obedience of Christ, the Anointed One, and His anointing.

Finally, Revelation 12:10–11 says that we overcome by the "blood of the Lamb and the Word of our testimony," the word of our confession of faith.

CHAPTER 8

Proclamation

Matthew 6:13b (NKJV) says: *For thine is the kingdom, and the power, and the glory, for ever. Amen.*

This is shouting ground! This is a place of proclaiming God's kingdom reigns in us and His kingdom endures forever and ever.

Romans 5:17 (NKJV) says: *For if by one man's offence death reigned by one; much more they which receive abundance of grace and of the gift of righteousness shall reign in life by one, Jesus Christ.*

Kingdom speaks of dominion and rule. A king rules or exerts power and authority or dominion with words. Remember the first thing God said to Adam (man) after He created him, in His image and likeness, was *And God blessed them and said to them, Be fruitful, multiply, and fill the earth, and subdue it [using all its vast resources in the service of God and man]; and* have dominion *over the fish of the sea, the birds of the air, and over every living creature that moves upon the earth* (Genesis 1:28 AMPC, emphasis mine).

God gave dominion or rule over all the works of His hands to Adam (man), and Adam was to rule and to subdue it, bringing it all under his control and leadership in service to God and for the benefit of mankind.

In Christ Jesus, the last Adam, we were redeemed and delivered from sin's dominion, from the kingdom and dominion of darkness, through His resurrection life.

Revelation 5:5–10 (AMPC) says

Then one of the elders [of the heavenly Sanhedrin] said to me, Stop weeping! See, the Lion of the tribe of Judah, the Root (Source) of David, has won (has overcome and conquered)! He can open the scroll and break its seven seals! [Gen. 49:9, 10; Isa. 11:1, 10; Rev. 22:16]

And there between the throne and the four living creatures (beings) and among the elders [of the heavenly Sanhedrin] I saw a Lamb standing, as though it had been slain, with seven horns and with seven eyes, which are the seven Spirits of God [the sevenfold Holy Spirit] Who have been sent [on duty far and wide] into all the earth. [Isa. 53:7; Zech. 3:8, 9 and 4:10]

He then went and took the scroll from the right hand of Him Who sat on the throne.

And when He had taken the scroll, the four living creatures and the twenty-four elders [of the heavenly Sanhedrin] prostrated themselves before the Lamb. Each was holding a harp (lute or guitar), and they had golden bowls full of incense (fragrant spices and gums for burning), which are the prayers of God's people (the saints).

And [now] they sing a new song, saying, You are worthy to take the scroll and to break the seals that are on it, for You were slain (sacrificed), and with Your blood You purchased men unto God from every tribe and language and people and nation. [Ps. 33:3]

And You have made them a kingdom (royal race) and priests to our God, and they shall reign [as kings] over the earth! [Exod. 19:6; Isa. 61:6]

So worthy is the Lamb to receive honor and glory and power forever and ever because He has purchased and redeemed us by His blood out of every tribe and language and people and nation. He has made us a kingdom, a royal race and priests to our God, and as kings, we shall reign with Him, the King of kings over the earth!

Isaiah 61:6 (AMPC) says: *But you shall be called the priests of the Lord; people will speak of you as the ministers of our God. You shall eat the wealth of the nations, and the glory [once that of your captors] shall be yours.*

Revelation 22:16–17 (NKJV) says

> *I, Jesus, have sent My angel to testify to you these things in the churches. I am the Root and the Offspring of David, the Bright and Morning Star.*
>
> *And the Spirit and [Rev. 21:2, 9] the bride say, "Come!" And let him who hears say, "Come!" And let him who thirsts come. Whoever desires, let him take the water of life freely.*

Revelation 15:3–4 (NKJV) says

> *They sing the song of Moses, the servant of God, and the song of the Lamb, saying:*
> *"Great and marvelous are Your works,*
> *Lord God Almighty! Just and true are Your ways, O King of the saints!*
> *Who shall not fear You, O Lord, and glorify Your name? For You alone are holy. For all nations shall come and worship before You, For Your judgments have been manifested."*

All honor, all glory, all power to You.
There is none other like You, O' Lord.
There is none above You.
There is none before You.
There is none beside You.
O' Lord, for You alone are worthy,
And of Your kingdom reign,
There will be no end. Amen!

ABOUT THE AUTHOR

Dennis Bos has long been a student of God's Word, studying and digging out spiritual truths to apply to daily life. He is a 1984 graduate of Rhema Bible College, Broken Arrow, Oklahoma, and a 1986 graduate of the School of the Local Church at Grace Fellowship, Broken Arrow, Oklahoma, under Pastor Bob Yandian and Dir. Geoff Jackson.

He spent several years at Grace Fellowship teaching a Sunday school class of sixty to sixty-five four-year-olds, developing ways to make God's Word understandable on the most basic level. He also worked with Youth Pastor Greg Ball at Grace Fellowship for two-and-a-half years in the "Rads for Christ" youth group.

Dennis later was the associate pastor at Mandate Christian Center, Smith Center, Kansas, under Pastor Jon "Rusty" Henderson and was the director of Children's and Youth Ministries from 1988 to 1989.

Dennis founded and pastored the Living Word Church of Osborne in early 1990 through 1995. At that time he closed the church and traveled full-time after most members had moved out of the area.

In 1991 Dennis traveled, on an independent short-term missions trip, to the USSR to St. Petersburg, Russia, to take Sunday school supplies, Russian Bibles, and teaching materials to the Russian people and to several of the Russian Orthodox churches in and around St. Petersburg.

In 2006 Dennis went to Iraq, working as a contractor with the DOD and US Army where he interacted with and held Bible studies among other contractors and soldiers. He remained in Iraq working with hundreds of soldiers, expats, and foreign nationals until August 2010.